# Iraqi Brush

Paintings by Fatimah Al-Asadi

Copyright © 2016 Fatimah Al-Asadi

All rights reserved.

ISBN-10: 1532950012
ISBN-13: 978-1532950018

# FATIMAH AL-ASADI

| | |
|---|---|
| Fatimah Al-Asadi | فاطمة الأسدي |
| Master's Degree in Linguistics | ماجستير لغة انكليزية / جامعة بغداد |
| PhD in curriculum design / university of Wyoming - USA | دكتوراه في تصميم مناهج اللغة الانكليزية / جامعة وايومنغ – الولايات المتحدة الامريكية |
| Exhibitions | المعارض |
| Annual Exhibit of the University of Baghdad, 2010 | المعرض السنوي لجامعة بغداد 2010 |
| Annual Exhibit of the College of Education – Ibn Rushd, 2010 | المعرض السنوي لكلية التربية / ابن رشد 2010 |
| Art Exhibit at the US Embassy in Baghdad, 2012 | معرض الرسم في سفارة الولايات المتحدة في بغداد 2012 |
| Arts and Stamps Exhibit at the US Embassy in Baghdad, 2013 | معرض الفن والطوابع في سفارة الولايات المتحدة في بغداد 2013 |
| Zainab: Arabic Media Exhibit, 2015 | زينب: سيدة الاعلام العربي، بغداد 2015 |

BAGHDADIAT

## ADAM & EVE

CRIMSON BENDING

## LANTERNS

GLORY

## SUNSET IN AFRICA

OLD CRAFT

QUIET NATURE

FOLKLORE

MOUNTAINS

LISTENING TO NATURE

WATERFALL

A LAKE

AT THE FOOT OF THE MOUNTAIN

ZAINAB: THE MOUNTAIN OF PAITIENCE

FARMS

BARN

A SHY MOON

THE DARK WOOD

A HOUSE IN SPRING

OLD TRUNKS

MOON LIGHT

SUNFLOWERS

THE SLAYED ROSE

PINKY SPRING

SNOWY RANGE

ROOFS

ORCHARD

A CALM NIGHT

AL-KHIDHIR CANDLES

A MAGIC BIRD

ZAKARIYA

MIHRAB MARTYR

FOLLIAGE

WINTER STORM

GREENARIES

THE ROSE OF THE SOUTH

## ABOUT THE AUTHOR

Fatimah is a PhD candidate at the University of Wyoming. She had her Master's degree in Linguistics from the University of Baghdad in which she taught for four years. She participated in the Fulbright program in 2011 in Bluefield State College in West Virginia. She has one novel, two collections of short stories, and one poetry book published in the United States. She published several research papers in recognized international and U.S. journals. She is working on two novels in English and three other ones in Arabic.

www.ingramcontent.com/pod-product-compliance
Lightning Source LLC
Chambersburg PA
CBHW050356180526
45159CB00005B/2036